Walk the World Proudly

ALSO BY HELEN LOWRIE MARSHALL

Close to the Heart
Bright Horizons
Dare to be Happy
Aim for a Star
Hold to Your Dream
The Gift of Wonder

Walk the World Proudly

❧ ❧

HELEN LOWRIE MARSHALL

Illustrated by William Goldsmith

❧ ❧

Doubleday & Company, Inc., Garden City, New York

1969

Dedicated to
First Lieutenant Edward Reynolds Naylor, Jr.
who gave his life in Vietnam
for freedom

Library of Congress Catalog Card Number 69–15210
Copyright © 1969 by Helen Lowrie Marshall
All Rights Reserved
Printed in the United States of America
First Edition

Contents

Walk the World Proudly

Walk the world proudly! Whoever you are,
You're a soul out of space sent to grace this earth-star,
A soul sent from Heaven with power and worth
To create a bit of that Heaven on earth.

Walk the world proudly—you're king of your life!
Empowered to conquer contention and strife,
Forces within you of measureless scope—
Eternal forces of faith, love, and hope.

Walk the world proudly—but walk with love, too,
For you have a mission entrusted to you
To lift those who stumble and those who would plod,
That they, too, may walk as a proud Child of God!

How Good It Is

What a good thing it is that hope lives on
    Deep in our heart of hearts;
What a good thing it is to find ourselves
    Singing when music starts.

What a very good thing it is that when
    The Creator concocted man,
He threw in a dash of humor just
    To spice His practical plan.

How wonderful it is that love
    Can be the driving power
To shape and rule these lives of ours
    Through every waking hour.

What a glorious thing it is that men
    Are not like peas in a pod,
But each in his individual way
    The image of his God.

You're Wonderful

You're wonderful! Oh yes, you are,
    And not alone to me,
For wonderful it surely is
    That one should even be!

A living, breathing, feeling, thinking,
    Laughing, loving you—
Could there be anything more purely
    Wonderful come true?

Oh yes, you're wonderful—and I
    And all men everywhere
Who, in this awesome thing called life,
    Have been allowed to share.

Blest with a heart and mind and soul
    And store of memory—
There's no more wondrous thing on earth
    Than you, my friend, and me.

I Would Rather

I would rather stumble a thousand times
    Attempting to reach a goal,
Than sit with the crowd in my weatherproof shroud,
    A shriveled, self-satisfied soul.

I would rather be doing and daring
    All of my error-filled days,
Than watching and waiting and dying,
    Smug in my perfect ways.

I would rather wonder and blunder,
    Stumbling blindly ahead,
Than for safety's sake, lest I make a mistake,
    Be sure and secure—and dead.

A Bit of Doing

It takes a bit of doing
    To make a dream come true.
The dream provides the starter,
    But the rest is up to you.

It takes determination
    To fight until you win.
The world has far too many folk
    With dreams that "might have been,"

Too many lazy wishers
    Who sit around and whine,
"I might have lived a life worthwhile;
    Once such a dream was mine."

It takes a bit of doing,
    But a dream that's given you
Is worth all you can give it
    To make that dream come true.

A Dream Is Not a Lowly Thing

A dream should be a sky-borne thing,
A distant, beckoning, high-borne thing,
On wings of Faith and Hope to ride the skies.
It should not be an earth-bound thing,
A limited and girth-bound thing,
Denied by doubt and fear its power to rise.

It ought to be a far-flung thing,
A soaring, shining, star-strung thing,
Unhampered by the downward pull of fears;
A hopeful, doubt-defying thing,
A trusting, God-relying thing,
A beacon growing brighter down the years.

A dream should be a treasured thing,
A sacred, Heaven-measured thing,
To give all life a purpose and a goal;
A dream is not a lowly thing—
A dream's a high and holy thing,
A God-inspired vision of the soul.

The God in Man

Something there is within man's soul
    That marches ever on,
Star-guided through the dark of night
    Toward the light and dawn.

Some urgency demands he seek
    A better way to go.
So long as there are dreams to dream,
    So long will mankind grow.

Something there is—the God in man—
    That strains for its release,
And will not settle for the less
    Than freedom, love, and peace.

This, Too, is Real

Again and yet again we hear it said
That sin has taken over—God is dead.
We see the turmoil in the world, the strife,
The sinister irreverence for life,
The senseless crime, the violence, the hate,
Man's own degrading of his high estate.
We're told that this is Truth; that we, today,
Must look at life the realistic way.

But I have seen the glory of the dawn,
And I have watched the sun's rays set upon
A world of twilight hushed to gentle rest;
I've seen a purple mountain's snow-capped crest;
I've planted roses—watched their buds unfold;
I've seen the tranquil faith of one grown old;
I've seen the splendid questing of the young
Pursuing dreams, unheralded, unsung.
I've watched the lovelight in a mother's eyes;
I've thrilled to starlight in a winter's skies—

God is not dead—He's all around us still.
The good and true and fine outweigh the ill.
There's beauty all about to see and feel—
And oh, my friend, this too, this too, is real.

Look Again

Look again—it's there somewhere,
    That beauty that you missed,
That high nobility with which
    Your youth had made a tryst.

It may be covered over now
    With ugliness and strife,
But love and human dignity
    Are still a part of life.

You have to look above, beyond,
    Down under and around,
But beauty, truth, and things of honest
    Worth can still be found.

So look again—keep looking—
    Never let your searching cease.
A firm belief in good and God
    Is man's one hope of peace.

Spirits on Parade

Every single word we speak,
    Every action made,
Every little interest puts
    Our spirits on parade.

What we really are shows through
    The social mask we wear;
The light of truth along life's way
    Reveals our real self there.

The spirit marches on—in stride—
    Or shuffles aimlessly—
But every soul is on parade
    For all the world to see.

Every spirit marches to
    The beat of his own drum,
The music that he chooses
    And the measure of its strum.

May a beat, triumphant, mark
    A stirring tempo played
With joyous, ringing cadence
    For *your* spirit on parade!

Let Life In

Let life in—don't hold it at bay,
This wide lovely world at your doorstep today—
This world of adventure, of challenge and love,
A world of more joy than you've ever dreamed of.

Open your heart to its rapture and pain,
The warmth of its sunshine, the cool of its rain;
Give your soul air, let it breathe, let it grow,
Live to the fullest this life here below.

Open your door as a haven to others,
Know the deep pleasure of serving your brothers.
Open your eyes and your ears and your mind—
Gather it in—all the truth you can find.

Welcome its beauty, be grateful, be glad—
Earn the good things of life, learn from the bad.
Let it all in—its contentment, its strife—
Live it and love it—this great gift of Life!

Starbath

When endless little duties
Close me in like airless walls;
When all the busyness of life
My baffled soul appalls;

It's good to find a hilltop,
High and quiet in the night,
And lift my eyes to Heaven
As the stars come into sight.

It's good to stretch my soul and mind
To vistas wide and far
Until I feel a oneness
With the farthest twinkling star.

Refreshed by this communion
With that greater God I find,
I come back from my starbath
Glad of heart and clear of mind.

Frustrations turn to challenge
As I take up life again,
So glad to be a part of God's
Great world of stars and men.

God Dreamed a Wondrous Dream

God dreamed a wondrous dream for you and me—
A world of peace and quiet harmony;
But you and I, with clumsy feet of clay,
Have made His dream a travesty today.
We wage our little wars—and lives are lost,
With innocence and youth charged with the cost.
We quarrel over petty statements said—
And on His fields of beauty lie the dead.
We fear and hate and rob and kill and cheat—
And crush His roses under marching feet.
God dreamed a wondrous dream. Perhaps, some day,
We'll try to make that dream come true His way.

Organs of Vision

Within the eye, a nerve so small
    A feather would outweigh,
Yet it brings into view the stars
    Ten billion miles away.

Just so, within the heart, the eye
    Of faith brings into sight
The unseen stars of glory
    In a world of truth and light.

The Comfort of Prayer

My heart often whispers a silent prayer
    In the midst of a noisy street,
For I know that the God I turn to is there
    As in the most quiet retreat.

My heart often murmurs a word of praise
    As I join in life's scurrying throng,
For I know that He follows the crowded ways
    And hears every heart's silent song.

My heart often holds up its empty cup,
    Drained dry by confusion and care,
For I know that I only need look up
    To be filled with the comfort of prayer.

Far and Near

Prayer is a powerful telescope
    That lets the eye see far
To the star of things as they ought to be
    From the land of things as they are.
And prayer, too, is a microscope
    That lets the eye see near
And count the worth of things of earth
    The heart holds close and dear.

Answered Prayer

I prayed for patience—and my prayer came true,
    For many tasks were given me to do,
Demanding patience I had never known.
    Each task completed found my patience grown.

I prayed for character and strength of soul,
    Unmindful of the costly, bitter toll;
And there was pain to bear, and there were tears—
    And character grown stronger down the years.

I prayed for inward peace of heart and mind,
    A comfort I could never seem to find
Till life compelled my thoughts to turn to others,
    And peace I found in service to my brothers.

A Promise Made

Be careful what you promise God—
    He'll take you at your word.
You may forget the prayer you said
    Or think it wasn't heard,
But some day when the time is right
    The door will open wide
And, hardly knowing how or why,
    You'll find yourself inside.

You'll find yourself conforming
    To that promise that you made,
For God believes in promises—
    His own are always paid.
And He believes in you and has
    Respect for what you say—
So take care what you promise
    And be prepared to pay.

Prayer Is a Medley

Prayer is a mixture of words and of working,
Thinking and acting, and promises made;
Dreaming and daring—and caring and sharing,
And following through with those promises paid.

Prayer is a medley of saying and doing,
Trying, denying, repenting, rebirth;
And inward and outward look at our living,
A revaluation of power and worth.

Prayer is a mingling of feeling and knowing,
A giving of thanks, an awareness of need;
Seeing, believing—and groping and growing
Higher and wider than dogma or creed.

Prayer is a union of faith and of reason,
A quelling of doubts, a resurgence of hope.
Prayer is the symphonic whole of our being,
The heartbeat of life in its noblest scope.

Remembered Gladness

Let remembered gladness
    Warm the day when cold winds blow.
Stir the embers in your heart
    And bask in their warm glow.

Stretch your soul's awareness
    Of the beautiful and fair.
Give your mind a well-earned rest
    From worry, toil, and care.

Think of only happy times
    And beauty that you've known,
Lovely deeds that may have sprung
    From seeds that you have sown.

Take a day's vacation,
    Let your mind relax and play
Among the sunny hours
    Of some happy yesterday.

Beyond the Trivial

Oh, the daily busyness
That robs life of its luster—
The littleness that causes us
To bicker and to bluster.
We build upon our little cares
And let our worries mount
Till we miss all the glory
Of the things that really count.

Oh, the smallness of our lives,
The shame that we should be
Content to fence ourselves away
From life's nobility;
Content to keep our eyes upon
Our own small plot of ground
When glorious adventure
Lies in waiting all around.

Oh, the satisfaction—
If we could only know—
Of stretching out beyond ourselves
And letting ourselves grow
Beyond our little fenced-in plot
Of triviality
To join that great adventure
Life on earth was meant to be.

Let There Be Light

Let there be light—there is enough
Of dark along life's way;
Let there be warmth and sunshine,
Let there be dawn and day.

Let there be little children,
Let there be kites on strings,
Clowns and monkeys, and birthday cakes,
And gardens with small growing things.

Let there be music and dancing,
Let there be moonlit skies,
Let there be youth and romancing—
Lovers with stars in their eyes.

Let there be woods in September,
Let there be lilacs in spring,
Bright winter days to remember—
Let there be songs to sing.

Let there be peace and forgiving
With faith in the Father above—
Let there be triumphant living—
Let there be light—and love!

God Bring the Spring

God bring the Spring to this old world,
    So bound with icy hate,
The warming sun of brotherhood,
    Its cold winds to abate.

God bring the miracle of Spring,
    The promise of new life,
The fresh, still dews of quietness
    On bitterness and strife.

God plant the pulsing seeds of love
    Within the hearts of men
That they may end the winter's wars—
    God bring the Spring again.

When and Where I Can

Dear God, please give to me to see
    The things that I can do,
The ways that I can spend my time
    And self in serving You.

Let me accept the challenge
    Of those things within my power
To bring about a better world
    In this, my little hour.

And give me understanding, too,
    That I may know and see
What lies beyond the limits
    Of the powers given me.

Let me not be envious of those
    Who mountains move,
But let me wield my ounce of strength
    For Thee with grateful love.

Not holding back for those whose skill
    And talents mine outspan,
But with such gifts as may be mine
    Serve when and where I can.

The Other Side of the World

Just on the other side of the world—
    The world of civilized din—
Is a little glade of cool green shade
    That begs me enter in.

Just a step on the yonder side
    Of the world's great bustling street—
It's waiting there, serene and fair,
    A gentle, hushed retreat.

A quiet sanctuary where
    The birds alone converse,
And I find peace within myself
    And with God's universe.

Just on the other side of the world—
    Oh, well within heart-call—
The green grass grows and a soft breeze blows,
    And it's not far away at all.

The Homestretch

I remember my Grandfather saying
In the days of the horse-drawn wheels,
When they turned the corner that led to home
The horse would pick up its heels
And fairly gallop toward the end,
So happy was he to see
The old familiar landmarks
Of that place he loved to be.

I often think how like that horse
Our life is here on earth,
How time keeps going faster
From the moment of our birth;
And when we're on the homestretch,
How the hours gallop on
As though the soul could hardly wait
To reach that Home beyond.

That tugging at the heartstrings
For the home that we hold dear
Seems transferred toward our Heavenly Home
The closer we draw near.

A Lonesome Place

There's a lonesome place against the sky
    Where sometimes all alone
We stand and watch the world go by—
    A strange world not our own.

For deep, heartbreaking sorrow
    We never fully share.
Alone we stand on that bleak hill,
    Lost in our deep despair.

But the cry that comes from a burdened heart
    Is heard—there is peace if we will,
For God's own Son knew the dreadful pain
    Of a cross on a lonesome hill.

He understands and He stands by
    With comfort in our grief,
To ease the pain and bring new hope
    And give the heart relief.

There is a lonesome place and all
    Must stand there now and then,
But if we place our hand in His,
    He'll help us smile again.

Wherever He May Be

He never seemed so young as when
He joined the ranks of fighting men;
And though my heart, rebellious, cried,
I felt a mother's fierce pride
That his ingrained belief in right
Was one for which he had to fight.

To him, injustice was the foe;
It left him no choice but to go.
He laughed it off, as youngsters do,
But that belief ran deep, I knew.
And though my eyes with tears were dim,
I was so proud, so proud of him!

He gave his life for that belief,
And I am proud, still, in my grief.
The fighting's finished for him there—
Mine just begun against despair.
Dear God, wherever he may be,
Help me to make him proud of me.

Beyond Reason

There is no answer to the question—"Why?";
The mystery of death defies the mind;
Such comfort as in reason souls would find,
Forever veiled and screened from mortal eye.
To understand it all we can but try,
At best to grope as go the wavering blind,
Awed by this dark that terrifies mankind,
In quest of some faint ray to clarify.
There is no reasoning that can condole
The sorrow-laden heart that seeks relief,
But faith there is, inborn within the soul—
A faith and hope that rise above all grief;
Faith in a life beyond the death-bell's toll,
And hope that finds its way to deep belief.

Via Dolorosa

I walked the street of sorrows,
    Leading to Golgotha's hill—
The Via Dolorosa,
    Echoing His footsteps still.

The day was gray with sadness,
    The shades of grief were there,
The echo of His agony
    Lay heavy on the air.

But then a sound broke through the gray,
    A sun's ray filtered through—
The laughter of a little child
    Turned somber skies to blue.

The Via Dolorosa,
    Street of sorrows, street of pain,
Became the Road to Heaven
    Where my Master lives again.

Let Your Heart Run Ahead

Let your heart run ahead to the Spring when life
    Bogs down in the winter's snow;
Let your heart run ahead where the warming breeze
    Coaxes new faith to grow.

Let your mind run ahead to the morning sun
    When the shadows crowd about;
Let your thoughts run ahead where the light of hope
    Breaks through the dark of doubt.

Let your heart run ahead and follow its lead
    To the land where meadowlarks sing
And flowers bloom and the world's in tune—
    Let your heart run ahead to the Spring.

Purple Promises

I must have a lilac tree,
    The sweet old-fashioned kind,
To bring the Spring again to this
    Grief-wintered heart and mind.

I must plant a lilac tree
    Beside the garden gate
To help me watch for Spring again
    Through this long winter's wait.

I must have a lilac's purple
    Promises to tell
My winter-weary soul that Spring
    Has come and all is well.

Without a God

There's so much beauty everywhere,
I could not bear it without prayer.
I could not bear it not to know
That Someone, somewhere, planned it so.
I think my heart would burst in two
Without a God to give thanks to.

God Must Love Beauty

God must love beauty, or why would He
Have put pink blooms on an apple tree?
Surely, He'd never have bothered to grow
A rose if He hadn't loved beauty so.
He wouldn't have planted a wooded hill,
Or planned the call of a whippoorwill,
Or splashed a sunset across the sky,
Or painted the wings of a butterfly.
He wouldn't have fashioned all this unless
He truly loved beauty and loveliness.

Marigolds

Marigolds I love and always will.
There's something fine and brave the way they stay
And keep on blooming, blooming, blooming still,
Long after other flowers fade away.
There's something that demands that I admire
Their golden sunniness, their high-held heads,
As though their very will points each one higher
To make up for the dreary frost-killed beds.

The Sky of Our Life

The sky of our life is an open sky,
    But only as wide as we will it;
The sky of our life is a star-filled sky,
    But only as full as we fill it.

For the sky of our life is bounded by love,
    And its stars are the glowing beams
Reflecting their light from the width and the height
    Of the heart's desires and dreams.

The sky of our life is a clear, blue sky,
    As blue as we let it be,
As clear and as open, as lovely and wide
    As the eyes of our soul can see.

The Commonplace

Thank the good Lord for the commonplace,
The thousand and one little ways
That lend a contentment and gladness and warmth
To all of our everydays.
Thank the great Giver of happy gifts—
Of sunshine and rain and snow,
Of flowers and books and families and friends
And every love we know.

A Basic Day

This was a basic day—a day
Of plain and wholesome living,
A balanced day of work and play—
Of getting and of giving.

Today was such a basic day
As Heaven's patterned after,
With simple lines that live alway
Of quiet love and laughter.

Awareness

Awareness, I think, is a part of love,
    A stirring that's felt in the heart,
With all of the exquisite rapture and pain
    Ascribed to a cupid's dart.

The heart aware is a heart in love
    With life. Its quickening beat
Responds to the beautiful, good, and true,
    As though to caresses sweet.

Awareness is surely the bride of life,
    As, joyfully clasping life's hand,
With infinite trust it opens the door
    To a love-crowned wonderland.

No God?

No God, you say? Perhaps you're right;
I have no mystic, deep insight,
No knowledge of theology
To prove that God exists for me.
But oh, the beauty of the hour
When winter's buds burst into flower
And fragrance fills the springtime breeze—
No God? Then who makes apple trees?

Think Before You Speak

Do we have an eye for beginnings?
Do we sense what results there could be?
Do we stifle the mischief before it takes root
And grows to maturity?

Do we have an awareness of buddings?
Does our heart see the full-blown flower—
The smile or the sigh that may bloom bye and bye
From the bud of this memory's hour?

Do we follow the time-proven adage,
And think before we speak—
Picture the harm that might be caused,
The trouble our words might wreak?

For the essence and mark of true wisdom,
The source of a happy heart,
Is the power to see what the outcome could be
And nip the bad buds at their start.

Trouble

You're very young, my dear, to sorrow so.
This grief of yours is very real, I know,
And if I told you now that you'd forget;
That you and Trouble, here, have scarcely met,
I'm very sure that you would not believe;
Nor if I said you're not the first to grieve
Because you found your tinsel was not gold.
But you are young, and Trouble's very old,
And wiser, kinder even, than you know.
Believe me, dear, although it hurts you so,
Some day you may look back, before life's end,
And know this Trouble truly was your friend.

Begin Again

Begin again—you can, you know.
Seek out a better way to go.
Forget the past—the past is dead,
And all Tomorrow lies ahead!
There's never a time too late to start
To bring to fruition that dream in your heart.
Begin again now, this minute, this day!
A new life is waiting—don't wish it away.

Trails Ahead

Many a lonely grave was left
Beside those trails west-bound.
Many a sorrowing heart, bereft,
Wept by a new-made mound.

But the wagon train moved out and on
To that new life ahead.
They started afresh at the break of dawn
And said goodbye to their dead.

Each of us has our prairie trail,
Our dead past with its cross,
The tragic errors that we bewail,
The hours we count as loss.

But we cannot camp beside defeat,
Crushed by the blows of Fate,
Heaping the mound that covers our loss
With bitterness and with hate.

The wagon train of life moves on
Away from the days that are dead,
And if we are wise we will bury the past
And look to the trail ahead.

Listen With Your Heart

Listen with your heart if you would hear
Harmony in those things near and dear,
Melody of memory's distant bells,
Song of hope that from the spirit wells.

Listen with your heart in quietness;
Yield your tired mind to the caress
Of healing thoughts of lovely things and fair,
The silent, gentle canticle of prayer.

Listen with your heart if you would be
At joyous one with God's great symphony.

Inward Peace

She had an inward peace. Tranquility
Glowed in her eyes as softest candlelight.
She was a garden spot at set of sun,
A hand upon a fevered brow at night.
The fire of a youth that once had been
Had settled to a quiet ember-glow.
She was a gentle, soothing lullaby,
A song at twilight, softly sung and low.

Musical Memories

Music creates memories
That sweeten with the years.
Some are wrapped in laughter—
Some are tied with tears.

Lullabies our mothers sang,
What memories recall;
And how we love those childhood airs
We sang when we were small.

The old school songs (more noise than tune!)
We sang so lustily,
Take on an almost reverent air,
So loved their memory.

The songs we sang as young folks—
What new tunes can compare
With those we used to harmonize
When Spring was everywhere!

Yes, music creates memories
That mellow with the years—
Some still bright with laughter,
Some still warm with tears.

The Art of Making-Do

When we were young we never knew
    What it was to be poor,
Though now I know the old wolf
    Must have camped beside our door.
But those frustrations caused by lack
    Of wealth, we never knew,
For very early we were taught
    The art of making-do.

We learned to use the things we had,
    Plus our imagination—
And what a wealth of happiness
    We found in our creation.
We watched our parents use the art—
    A craft they dignified
With ingenuity that fed
    Our honest family pride.

And that resourcefulness we learned,
    Has served us well these years;
Belief in one's own powers tends to
    Minimize life's fears.
Our children have a great deal more
    Than we, as youngsters, knew—
But they've been cheated of the art
    And fun of making-do.

First Love

You live in a wonderful world of your own,
My beautiful stranger—my little girl grown—
A world full of dreams, full of newness and joy,
A world peopled largely right now by one boy.

You smile condescendingly down from your star
On all earthly mortals who can't reach that far;
With touching compassion for all here below
Who haven't a knight like your own bashful beau.

My beautiful Princess, my little girl grown,
You'd never believe such a first love was known
Not too many moons ago, and by none other
Than I, your adoring, but stupid, old mother.

Take Care

It rather behooves us all, I think,
To take care how we tread,
Lest we dislodge the halo
Love has placed upon our head.

Cabin for Sale

We bought a cabin in the hills
    For rest and relaxation.
It needed fixing up a bit
    So that was our vacation.
We pacified our aching backs
    And muscles, bruised and battered,
With dreams of lazy long weekends—
    How soon those dreams were shattered!

Before the paint was dry, unbidden
    Guests began descending,
One by one, or ten by ten,
    All happily weekending.
Next-door neighbors, relatives,
    Old friends from distant places,
Even slight acquaintances
    With unfamiliar faces.

We fetched and carried, cooked and cleaned
    From Friday night through Sunday,
And staggered back to work again,
    A total wreck each Monday. . . .
We've put our cabin up for sale.
    Should we crave mountain air,
We still have friends with cabins
    And we'll spend our weekends there.

Devout Avower

Each New Year's Day I make
A solemn vow that I'll abstain
From anything that has
A tendency to make me gain.

I vow to exercise each day
With program firm and rigid,
And take long walks, no matter
Be the weather hot or frigid.

I repeat these solemn vows
Each time my bulging figure
Necessitates my purchasing
A new dress one size bigger.

I vow it all again each time
I step upon the scales.
The sobering effect of this
Procedure never fails.

Without a doubt there never was
A more devout avower—
So full of good intentions,
And so lacking in will power!

Class Reunion

Our fiftieth reunion
Was a glorious affair—
The girls were portly matrons now,
The boys had lost their hair,

But we were very close—
In fact, we had to be to see
The nameplates that provided us
With instant memory!

The ghosts of Yesterday were there,
A wistful searching party,
Only half-concealed by manner
Just a shade too hearty.

A whole roomful of strangers
Slapping backs, exchanging quips—
Bewildered disillusionment
Behind the smiling lips.

Then, here and there, we'd hear an echo
From the long ago—
Some long-forgotten laugh or voice
We used to love and know.

And for a few short moments
The long half-century
Would slip away, as we relived
The days that used to be.

It was a great success, I guess,
But if the truth were told,
I felt a little out of place—
The rest were all so *old!*

Too Many

I simply can't see (and I know these views date me)
Why everyone has to congratulate me
On having a birthday. They know I'm unhappy
Enough without everyone going all sappy
And waggishly pounding my poor aching back
While gleefully shouting that corny old crack.
"Happy Birthday, you rascal!" they chortle and squeal,
"Remember you're only as old as you feel!"
If I were as old as I feel—oh, brother!
On birthdays I'm older than Whistler's grandmother.
Birthdays? No, thank you, I'm not having any—
They're lovely, I know, but I've just had *too many!*

Eating Crow

There's one thing I've learned, as older I grow—
That there's precious little I really know.
The vehement likes and dislikes I've declared,
The stubborn opinions I've mulishly aired—
I've since come to find that they aren't all so,
And time and again, I am forced to "eat crow."

With every new wrinkle and every gray hair,
I find I have fewer opinions to air;
Those doors of my mind that I closed with such force,
I now find myself looking on with remorse.
The things that I once vowed I never would do,
I catch myself doing—and liking them, too!

It's lucky for me the mere fact of old age
Entitles a person to be thought a sage.
If they only knew it, those years they revere
Are not quite the pedagogue they would appear.
About all they've taught me—and I've lived a few—
Is never to trust what appears to be true!

Aftermath

The sweetest pastime in the world—
    Speaking in first person—
(Though from the other fellow's viewpoint
    It's no doubt, the worst one)
Is to tell in gory bliss
    And gruesome conversation
The bloody details, one by one,
    Of one's own operation!

Imagination knows no bounds
    As you lie there in stitches,
Garbed in one of those awful gowns
    That has no back nor britches.
No subject is too delicate,
    All modesty takes flight,
As you launch out in rhapsody
    About your wretched plight!

Your story ends when visitors
    Begin to softly snore.
There's really not much fun
    In going on then any more.
It's obvious your audience
    Has no appreciation
Of all the finer things of life
    Like this—your operation.

Ker-Choo!

Now, I'm a sneezer—it's a trait
That grows on our family tree.
We're never content with just one sneeze
Or even as many as three;
And each is a splendid explosion
That stems from the tips of our toes.
None of this stuff that's discouraged
By a finger pressed under the nose!

I'd always accepted the sneezing
As part of one's natural fate,
And never considered the subject
A matter for any debate.
Then my better half—a non-sneezer—
Read in a book where it said
That the urge to sneeze is all mental—
In other words—all in your head.

When I sneeze now I feel guilty,
As though I'd committed a sin.
(Not that it makes any difference,
There's no way to hold the thing in.)
But now it's no great blast of triumph,
The way that a sneeze ought to be.
Instead, it's a meek, unobtrusive,
Apologetic "A-chee."

I wish that I knew who had authored
That book that my better half read.
I'll wager he hasn't one good honest sneeze
In the whole of his arrogant head.
He, too, is no doubt a non-sneezer,
Or he never could write of a sneeze
As a mere mental state to be turned on or off
At will with such nonchalant ease.

It's all in the head, he says. Granted.
But it's got to get out of there, too—
And the good Lord provided the answer—
A good, honest, rousing KER-CHOO!

Trite But Right

It would be so nice to do
Only what we wanted to,
But, as Grandma used to say,
"Character's not built that way."
And, although a trifle trite,
I'm afraid Grandma was right.

Patience, Patients

The cold and gloomy silence of the tomb
Has nothing on a doctor's waiting room,
Where patients sit, all dolefully about,
Wondering if the doctor's in or out.
You take the chair that's nearest to the door
And sit there, staring blankly at the floor.
When, finally, you simply aren't able
To stand the strain, you tiptoe to the table
Where magazines of ancient vintage lie.
You look them over, feeling every eye
Upon you, till in panic you retreat
Back to the seclusion of your seat,
There to find, with thoughts best left unsaid,
You've chosen one that you've already read.
And so you sit. The office clock's loud tick
Keeps repeating, "Sick—you're sick—you're sick,"
Till by the time they finally call your name
You're ever so much worse than when you came.
Yes sir, for sheer, unmitigated gloom,
There's nothing like a doctor's waiting room.

Second Grade Knight

Handsome? Well—no—but he had a grin
That showed where his two front teeth had been.
Well-groomed? Well, now, let's just say
He was more carefree and gay—
Wearing his clothes with charming ease,
Candid patches on seat and knees,
Sturdy shoes scuffed at the toes—
But who cared about his clothes!
He had a swagger a king would grudge,
That wonderful light of my life called Pudge.
Every recess he broke my heart
And his folks moved away so we had to part,
But he was my Robin Hood—I was his Maid—
Pudge—my Knight of the Second Grade.

A Boy and His Dog

Did you ever watch a small boy
With his dog exploring the wood?
It's a lesson in life at its purest,
A picture of absolute good.

The three of them—boy, dog, and nature—
No closer rapport could there be;
An hour of perfect enchantment,
Heart-whole and whole-heartedly free.

A boy and his dog and all nature—
No finer example is found
Of pure, unpretentious awareness
Of beauty, of sight, and of sound.

If only we oldsters could capture
One moment of that perfect hour
And store it away to draw on its peace
When the trials of life overpower.

Susie

They called her Susie—
    It was not her name,
But she was known as Susie
    Just the same.

Her children and their children
    Called her so,
And more endearing term
    I'll never know.

For love bestowed the name;
    The warmth and wit
Of deep affection made
    A crown of it.

A crown she wore with laughing
    Grace and pride—
The name her family's love
    Had glorified.

They called her Susie—
    Why—no one could tell,
But oh, it fit her sunny self
    So well.

Cicada Symphony

In the cool of the evening sit with me—
There's an orchestra in the old elm tree.
The "katy-did" chorus is in full swing;
You never have heard such practicing!
The leader must surely be very fine
To hold so many musicians in line.
There's only one fellow who lags a bit
And, no doubt, he will get over it.
Their grand finale, loud and clear,
Is really beautiful to hear—
Up the scale to the glorious top,
Then—as of one accord—they stop!
Do come over and sit with me—
It's a splendid concert—and all for free!

Chapel by the Road

A poem ought to be a little
    Chapel by the road,
Where souls can tarry for a while
    And ease their heavy load.

It ought to be a quiet sanctuary
    Where the heart
Can find a moment's respite from
    The busy world apart.

A bit of beauty standing by
    The dusty road of day
To cheer the weary traveler
    Along a brighter way.

As We Go

And now we ask God's blessing
As we go our separate ways;
May He walk beside and guide us
In the living of our days.

May He heighten our awareness
Of the good and true and fine,
And kindle humble gratitude
Within your heart and mine.

May He give our faith a substance
That the world can see and feel,
And may we put that faith to work
With love-inspired zeal.

May our trust in Him be strengthened
By each trial along the way,
As we go now with His blessing,
In whose blessed name we pray.